As for Dream

Also by Saskia Hamilton

POEMS

All Souls

Corridor

Canal: New and Selected Poems

Divide These

AS EDITOR

The Dolphin Letters, 1970–1979:
Elizabeth Hardwick, Robert Lowell, and Their Circle

The Dolphin: Two Versions, 1972–1973 by Robert Lowell

Words in Air: The Complete Correspondence between
Elizabeth Bishop and Robert Lowell (with Thomas Travisano)

The Letters of Robert Lowell

As for Dream

Saskia Hamilton

Graywolf Press

Publication of this volume is made possible in part by a grant provided by the Minnesota State Arts Board through an appropriation by the Minnesota State Legislature, and by a grant from the National Endowment for the Arts. Significant support has also been provided by the Bush Foundation; Dayton's Project Imagine with support from Target Foundation; the McKnight Foundation; a Grant made on behalf of the Stargazer Foundation; and other generous contributions from foundations, corporations, and individuals. To these organizations and individuals we offer our heartfelt thanks.

"Haiku" by Matsuo Bashō—used as an opening epigraph—from *The Essential Haiku: Versions of Bashō, Buson, & Issa,* edited and with an introduction by Robert Hass. Introduction and selection copyright © 1994 by Robert Hass. Unless otherwise noted, all translations copyright © 1994 by Robert Hass. Reprinted by permission of HarperCollins Publishers, Inc.

Published by Graywolf Press
212 Third Avenue North, Suite 485
Minneapolis, Minnesota 55401
All rights reserved.

www.graywolfpress.org

Published in the United States of America

ISBN 978-1-55597-316-2

Library of Congress Catalog Number: 00-101776

Cover art: Piero della Francesca, *The Dream of Constantine,* S. Francesco, Arezzo, Italy. Scala/Art Resource, New York.

Cover design: Julie Metz

Contents

I.

II.

III.

For Daniel Brush

Sick on a journey,
my dreams wander
the withered fields.

Bashō

I.

The Song in the Dream

The song itself had hinges. The clasp on the eighteenth-century Bible
had hinges, which creaked; when you released the catch,
the book would sigh and expand.

The song was of two wholes joined by hinges,
and I was worried about the joining, the spaces in between
the joints, the weight of each side straining them.

Late Winter Rain

Reverie is the word.

Reverence.

He is not attentive to you so you are not attentive to the world.

All it takes is one apology for you to wake up.
But it has to be the right apology.

In the Hospital

Will you hand me the bulbs?
I have to plant them, he said, but I can't reach them.

The attendant came in and adjusted a dial.
Still she did not get up from the chair.

You know, were his last words,
You really are very lazy.

Hunger

He was buried during the hunger winter. The ground was wet and not as soft as he had expected.

After the tulip bulb had boiled a long time, he had thought his knife would go through it easily and the pulp inside would be slightly pink, like the tips of the leaves of a young artichoke. But it was sweet, and not to be eaten, and scratched his throat.

Where he was now, nobody knew; but sometimes his daughter passed him in the street. And one summer, late in her life, she saw him at her house almost every day. He stood at the foot of her bed at night when she couldn't sleep, and couldn't tell

what it was he wanted.

So she talked to him and, when she ran out of things to say, she read aloud from her book. The only other sound in the house was the tick of small insects against the lamp-light.

End of Summer

What you are unable to make from this is what I want to eat.

What I am unable to make from this is what you want to eat.

Dream at Eighty-Four

Only when she sat down to write a letter did she remember:
She had to move, and she
hated it.

And when she came to the new house,
the first floor was so full of debris, she could hardly
wade through it.

At Eighty-Four

Her daughters felt like children on the days they came.
She wanted to say
it was too late to make amends—;

but the work of this lifetime and the next weigh the same.

And waking from the dream was making room for death.

In the Garden

In the back garden, the tree above us was thinning and sickly. She put the shears away and sat on the bench.

When her sister was dying of tuberculosis, she would read her letters on the balcony away from the children and then burn them. They were wrapped in layers of paper and sent from her mother, who wrote on the envelopes, "Enclosed is a letter from Anna."

Her sister, she said, fell in love with the doctor during the last years of her life. He helped her move into a little cottage on the grounds of the sanitarium, and she would lie all day in bed, in nightgowns that she embroidered very beautifully, and sew dresses for the children (which had to be cooked in a kind of oven before they were sent, so they were ruined), and write letters. Once the children came and were allowed to wave at her from the garden. This was one year before the war.

She often found she was in a long tunnel, walking in one direction or the other, reaching neither destination. One day she gave up her ambition to be a poet and the dream ended. She continued to write letters. The distinction was simply formal.

She was not able to work in the garden as long as she used to, but it was August, which meant that soon her daughter would come and they would pack up the house. The roses luxuriated. She renamed one bush *Madame Récamier.*

The House between Two Meadows

He had come too close. He was everywhere she walked, watching her while she listened politely to the tea-time conversation, reaching for her when she washed the dishes, lying beside her when she went to bed. He was floating just beyond the limits of her body, she almost kissed his lips when she drank from a glass, put her mouth on his jeans when she sat at the table to work.

Sometimes, when it seemed a longing so cloying and unsolvable, she would try to distract herself. But it wasn't until the rainstorm on the fifteenth of August that she understood anything.

Her aunt was making a bed and they were talking about books. The rain picked up and started to stream down the windows and the house was blanketed and suddenly quite small. She thought of the desk upstairs, the rain on the garden, so when they folded the blanket and laid it at the foot of the bed, she climbed the stairs and closed the door and sat down to work. A whole hour passed.

Who will help you? she thought. It's the weight of telling. Better read a different book. Better sleep with someone else. Better do anything than hold so still, you can almost feel him touching you.

At Eighty-Four

On the anniversary of your death
I did very little—worked in the garden,
had a glass of sherry at lunch-time with some crackers,
put on a cassette tape, and sat very still.
I wondered then if I was sad. No, not really.
And all at once I felt heat rushing through
me. I recognized you.

His Face

I can't quite recognize what I looked like as a child.

When I was small, Grandmother gave us chocolate and orange
slices at coffee-time. We were given
books to read. When I was small
I sat on the couch and kissed and
kissed my own hand.

There Is No Greater Love

When he woke from the dream, his face
was clean, as if light was rising from it.

He recalled two things:
the dead boy in the court, the breath yanked
out, like a bath-plug—

the dead boy in the court when he came
with the ambulance, the lady who yelled fuck you
as they lifted him, cops crowding down towards them;

and the striped halls of the teaching hospital,
he was waiting and waiting for tests,
black liquid in his body

and a phrase of Ben's going in his head.
But now he was dead.
He had lifted himself away from his body so

gently, he hadn't even noticed.

Sorrow in the Body

Just gallons of oil.
And the polished gears and levers
can't handle the volume coming up.

Black juice and boiled rice.
You're going to be here
way too long.

His Wife's Death

Around the corner the smell of illness,
medicine, used sheets, windows you can't open,
poverty outside which sickens you like the rattling of
a train window you can't rest your head on.

She lay there for weeks, dying, and you did manage
to care for her, though you often wanted her dead,
you wanted her well, you wanted the illness
to slip from the closed room,
you wanted to open the windows,
you never wanted to take the train to that place again.

A Vigil

She couldn't hear because she thought they were dead.

But she was the one who had died, and they sat
around the edges of the bed, a little dazed,
out of it (though they didn't want to be).

She is hearing a pinch-tree
pinching the breath out of her.

It Fled

It fled
from the one who was dead

and hid in you.

Someone Else

I was glad to make love to him not for the pleasure so much
as the pressure on my stomach to help me forget
the weight of what slept there.

A Story

There was the story of the car lying on its side
when the child came upon it.
This was the child's dream. The car was an angel
insofar as it was white and emitted light.
The papers scattered everywhere—the contents of a hundred over-
turned filing cabinets—lay untroubled on the pavement,
though it was clear to her what was written down
was terrible. What's scribbled in the body.
For the worst was inside her right side.
Nothing ever came again to warn her.

II.

Weight

You want a story? I'll give you one.
A dangerous man is inside of me; when I
sit still for ten minutes my breath plummets
lower and lower into my body like a fishing weight
that will eventually reach the end of my spine and I will
sit up straight or fall over onto the table.

The table has a part in the story, too,
you will find out later.

We are all waiting to hear
what the hook yanked-up from down there.

Early Winter

Frozen in one place and then the next.

There is mercury in my veins.
When it breaks up and scatters, each drop
carries the whole message. It doesn't really gain
from massing. It makes me want—;
no. It makes me want—;
no. It just
makes me sick about the whole thing.

To prove that I love you, I would carry you anywhere,
I would follow any bus down the worst road.
I would even forget you, if that would convince you.

Forget

Don't think that I never forgot him. I did.

I went to the couch and lay down, feeling a coagulated dullness that I knew was hiding the panic that must come soon.

I felt the cold of the stone floor move up my leg. Sneaky.

You Know the Way

What he wants from me is numb, it is crushed
inside the dark hole of the last place you'd ever look.

I have practiced dreaming. It works sometimes.
My heart is there, somewhere thrilling away.

I can't kiss anyone else for this reason.
And there's just the voice in my ear, which says:

I'm looking for one rusty black bike
one rusty thing to take me down the road

Winter Rain

The badger will live somewhere else.
The dog snuffled out its house.

The bird is crushed in the ice.
Fuck off. The winter says.

What little light there is rises
from the intricate, thorny tangle of branches,

and so you know

what's possible rises from the dark hedges,
the flat and empty landscape on the far

side. Winter brown, winter straw, winter rain
falling now on the field.

Wet. Better get yourself inside.

Waiting

Birds pass through your garden.
You buy new books and they pile up
without luster and you look at the garden
and sink deeper and deeper inside the tubular
body which repeats the shape of your heart.

For Want Of

I have to wake up again and again.

I have to take him and show him the gate.

Something unconscious yesterday lifted
the edges with a shovel and slipped in.
It wasn't alive, it was no living thing.

The light in the morning is yellow again.
Sky brooding in places, blue in places.
Heavy with intentions over the town.

Slow Train

When I was not in love I felt a poverty of images.
This is just a song. This is just craven
back-pedaling. This is no story
and no poem. When I was not in love I fell dumb.

When I was not in love a pain at the center
of my back was holding my breath
in a little sack where the ribs separate.
The gateway to the place that is unreachable.
Where the Sliding Delta rides right by my door.
Watching it pass from the front porch.
Cigarettes are no good, but they organize
a moment. That's their virtue.
I need an organizing principle.

Sooner old train you're going to care for me.

For Want Of

Like a bowl in your stomach.
Turn it over, it will scoop up
a lot of you. A lot of dried wings.

Pastoral

His delight was once to me what passed between us
for kissing.

After Catullus

You wicked girl, to have wanted him at all.
Does he know this? What if he knew this?

Another Stupid Party

I had to stand at the other end of the room
and talk to a hundred other people.

My longing for him trailed after
me and although its nature had not
changed, its agency had,

as if it were the angel whispering at the back of my head,
and if I turned I would see, on the floor behind me,
that we held each other, we kept insisting, always
working towards the end of the story,

his breath on me the weight of the dream I had
in which I kissed him and felt a skittish
animal slip in.

Tomorrow I'm going to do something about it.

The Next Day

Wet dog, wet porch, wet streets, old wet people
passing by. The angels are in another part of the city.
If you walked as he walks and breathed as he
breathes, you think, they might get interested again.

But one day you'll be back in your own body,
and although you'll be dead or asleep,
your hair, your teeth, and your nails

will flourish.

Legible Mystery

For no one understands the framework but you,
and they really want you to give a little.

Late Winter

Very strange, yellowy light this morning.
The sky absolutely white.

A storm is gathering that I try to keep from gathering in my house.

I don't know how to relate my longing
or tell a story so you'll see.

What I say is not true and you should not trust me.

When I have found it you will be able to tell
from the breath inside the language.

I used to think it was the cunning of sickness.
Now I think it is the cunning of love.

Listen

The flies are hovering over the barley,
a storm is pressing, the swallows are flying low.
His talk is shitty air itching your ear.
You just need some penicillin.
You just need one phrase to say over and over
to get him out from inside of you.

Last Errand

Tell me if you know what the truth is.
Far hills, the low houses, the dry no where.

No, what you were saying was
the only way to know.

You want it enacted here, on the tongue, in
the throat.

Dusk

It is hard to notice anyone else touching me.

I want to shovel sand into this ache and stopper my mouth and close my eyes

and slip

into another dream.

Just one more Monday, and by the next:

III.

Work

All night long, my body was hot and impossible to slow down.

Why do I say I can't do it? It's all I say to myself.

There is everything in the world to be done. Everything to prepare for.

November

There is a bright eye in me dulled by the activity of my dreaming eye.
One phrase going on for so long you don't hear anything anymore
but the breath it takes to say it.

There are many faces through which to address God.
Why would you stop? How could you speak against him?
There are many faces but you are not looking closely.

If, as you read this, he comes down the stairs on the other side of the ocean
and lights the stove—are either of you more alone, less
able to face your death, that you are not in the same room?

You need both eyes where you're going.

On the table you work at, stacks of paper,
a lamp, a scratch, a hole, and two passersby
talking outside, the fifth of
November in a city growing cold.

You did not know, you did not
know. Therefore, you changed.

Reverence

Your silence is so complete, I can hear it pull me from one end of the century
to the other.

The geese call themselves together for the journey.
The bells ring past the hour; they urge us on.
There is no alphabet for that sound.

If I said it right and deposited it in the whorl of your ear.
Do not echo so, do not echo thus.

What of it? Why do I trouble myself?
There is nothing left to be learned from those letterings.
Close the book. Winter is on its way, the city is waking.
Gray and surprisingly warm today.

Thirty-seven leaves left on the tree outside
and a whole day to make use of.

What's Past

Even if it is just a passing thought he has when he is driving north.

In my last dream about him, we were not supposed to be that close. He leaned
                                        his head near mine and I
touched it, but we were not looking at each other.

The Apology

The grief has its sources
but often moves in no relation to them. It
wants to touch everything. Whenever I see you,
I want to touch everything.

The Kiss

We hung the towels to dry and put the dishes away. The cellar smelled of the dull
stone floor,

but the kitchen smelled of pears, which were flecked with white
and sinking into themselves in the heat.

The Embrace

Light reached into the room, from time to time, when the wind parted the leaves,
                                                              like hands
parting a shirt.

                    And all I remember is standing in a doorway,

the shadows around the doorway, an early evening darkness in the house.

Waiting for the News

That night, she was tired of mothering. Not that she minded I was there,
                                                        necessarily;
but she was readying herself for death.

On the bookshelves, law textbooks and journals.

At ten-thirty, the phone rang with the news.

Later, lying in bed and looking out the window at the roofs of the city, I knew I
                                                would have to give up even
the only one I love. Soon, soon.

The room was perfumed by old books and shirts laundered for the one who
                                                                had gone.

In the City

We were having coffee two days after he died, a quiet morning,
the roar of the city a far-off animal,
the acacia trees in the park stirring, the wind
lifting the curtains and the edges of the tablecloth.

"I sometimes have the feeling," she said,
"that I don't belong anymore in my life."

Still

The still body emitting no heat or energy may explain
why things in the house filled with a kind of stuffing

that smelled sour and strange. No one knew
what to do, except climb up to the room

and look. The black spots first appeared
on the chin and then the hollow below the thumb,

like bruises. And then above the long dark box
hovered the light that had left the body.

The only disaster left took place in the small space
of your own. Until the day you asked yourself,

What's true? I will tell you.

Listen

The swallows rose from the fields and flew east from every direction. Flight patterns as efficient as the mind's.

—▪—

I have the ingredients of the dream in my hands in the morning.

Work

You were hired by the tools in the box and set to work.
How to hold a stone. How to throw it.

The project took a long time, you had to
learn to take care.

You were digging underground
and you didn't know where.

Sometimes it was a tunnel
and sometimes it was a stone.

—◦—

The first sign that summer was over was in the fields.

Barley stalks stood up from the earth, which was painted
in a black so thick you would choke if you ate it.

The wind pulled the rose branches and tore them from the wall.

It is time to pack up the house and carry yourself away.
The fields are filling with water.

—◦—

How will you render it, how will you hold it,
how will you bury it and carry on?

There is everything in the world still to do.

You spent so many years trying to find
the end of the day, the close of shop,
when the work goes back in the box.

He calls work the throat. I call work the chest.

But it is lower than that,
the drawer in the belly,
where the remnants are.

And when you open it, what will you find?
That it was neither the throat nor the chest.

It was the ear that led you this far.

Late Winter

What lingered like humidity in the memory of your dream
was him touching you and saying

something you didn't quite hear,

the dream like an ear in its intricacy,

like the weight of his body pressing you down,
the heavy blankets covering you,

or the ten years it took,
forgetting why you ever bothered,

before you understood anything.

And after you woke, out beyond the house,

winter brown, winter straw, winter rain,
the wind out of control.

Bruges

After coffee, we drove to the museum.
The streets were messy and cold. Our coats not sufficient.
The car wouldn't warm up and emitted great clouds from the exhaust.
The cold was a kind of gas that seeped through the doors
and windows and wrapped around my shoes.

Down a corridor into a forest of paintings,
there were no likenesses in the portraits, except a little owl,
a goose-creature beseeching St. Jerome.

The First Evening

Listen to that drumming, so light it skims along the surface
like the birds at dusk dipping down to the water,
or a nonsense rhyme going on below the song.

He sipped.

        Then the evening was over, even though
it was soft and if we were to go on we would reach the sea.

I wore red beneath my shirt.

What was to come?

There was a plank between my shoulder blades
leaning against the wall inside of me, waiting to be put to use by the workmen
who come at six and work until three.

Sleep while you can for tomorrow it will be morning.

Notes

As for Dream: The title is a translation of a phrase in Matsuo Bashō's last poem, written in the fall of 1694. The translation of the phrase and the poem are by Robert Hass (*The Essential Haiku*, Ecco Press, 1994).

At Eighty-Four: The poem owes a debt to Tomas Tranströmer.

There Is No Greater Love: Dedicated to Leslie Whitt Wetzonis (in memory of her father, Leon Whitt). The reference is to Ben Webster's recording of "There Is No Greater Love" (Black Lion Records, 1965).

For Want Of: Thanks to Rites of Spring for letting me borrow the title of a song from their first record (*Rites of Spring,* Dischord Records, 1984).

Another Stupid Party: The title is taken from a song by Mark Eitzel on the American Music Club's *California* (Frontier Records, 1988).

The Kiss: The poem owes a debt to Czesław Miłosz.

Bruges: Years after I wrote this poem, I returned to the gallery where I first saw these paintings. I discovered that paintings depicting scenes from the legends of St. Anthony and St. Jerome were hanging side by side. Readers familiar with the lives of the saints will recognize that the creature had leapt from one painting to another in my memory, inadvertently.

Acknowledgments

I am grateful to the foundations that administer the Beinecke Memorial Scholarships and the Ruth Lilly Poetry Fellowships, which supported my education; the board and staff of the Lannan Foundation; and editors of the following journals, in which some of these poems appeared (in earlier drafts): *Colorado Review, New England Review,* the *Plum Review, Salt,* and the *Threepenny Review.*

For suggestions, I am indebted to many friends—your work is visible here; but I would like to thank Joanna Picciotto and Robert Hass in particular for their close readings. And for their kindness at crucial junctures, I would also like to thank Stephen Booth, John Burghardt, Michael Burkard, Elizabeth Hardwick, the Hamilton family, and the familie Wiarda.

Saskia Hamilton (1967–2023) was the author of four collections of poetry, *As for Dream, Divide These, Corridor,* and *All Souls*. She was the editor of several volumes of poetry and letters, including *The Letters of Robert Lowell,* and was the co-editor of *Words in Air: The Complete Correspondence between Elizabeth Bishop and Robert Lowell*. Her edition of *The Dolphin Letters, 1970–1979: Elizabeth Hardwick, Robert Lowell, and Their Circle* received the Pegasus Award for Poetry Criticism from the Poetry Foundation and the Morton N. Cohen Award for a Distinguished Edition of Letters from the Modern Language Association. She was also the recipient of an Arts and Letters Award in Literature from the American Academy of Arts and Letters. She taught for many years at Barnard College.

As for Dream has been set in Stempel Garamond, a version of
the original Garamond designed by Claude Garamond
(or Garamont), one of several great typecutters in Paris
during the early sixteenth century.

Book design by Wendy Holdman.
Set in type by Stanton Publication Services, Inc.

Printed in the USA
CPSIA information can be obtained
at www.ICGtesting.com
LVHW08055215 0724
785510LV00003B/281